T0195968

ALWAYS BRIDGE

A memoir and tribute to include 8 women of uncommonly quiet strength and good humor over a 58-year period.

By Linda J. Palmer

Archway Publishing books may be ordered through booksellers or by contacting:

Archway Publishing
1663 Liberty Drive
Bloomington, IN 47403
www.archwaypublishing.com
844.669.3957

Because of the dynamic nature of the Internet, any web addresses or links contained in this book may have changed since publication and may no longer be valid. The views expressed in this work are solely those of the author and do not necessarily reflect the views of the publisher, and the publisher hereby disclaims any responsibility for them.

Any people depicted in stock imagery provided by Getty Images are models, and such images are being used for illustrative purposes only.
Certain stock imagery © Getty Images.

ISBN: 978-1-4808-9572-0 (sc)
ISBN: 978-1-4808-9573-7 (e)

Library of Congress Control Number: 2020917344

Print information available on the last page.

Archway Publishing rev. date: 10/29/2020

CHAPTER 1

We started off young; naive? Probably.

In the beginning there was just Yung and Jo (myself) shopping in the local Safeway for groceries on a Saturday. We were teachers at an elementary school in the small school district of a middle-class, even "provincial" town (that's what my son appropriately called it later). Saturday being a day off for us, we did our shopping and some kind of food preparation that day, often turning to a bridge game that night if we could talk our respective roommates into it. None of us were highly social partiers, though we occasionally went to "the city" for entertainment on a Saturday night.

If someone had a rare date (we were all but one single), she quickly said, "No thanks" to the bridge game. Ultimately, the bridge game became a Friday night way to "crash". We were at varying degrees of skill and never at that point into what I call "The Big Time" in bridge. The year was 1962. As teachers and administrators, we were selected to be there because of our competence as professionals. We loved teaching and the kids kept it interesting for us and hopefully we for them as well,

Edie, a co-teacher, was more senior than we, as was Hilda, our principal. Both were consummate educators and professionals, but also very companionable and even protective and nurturing. We had a lot of fun together. Hilda was under the gun the year that I came, with 9 new teachers of 18 teaching staff. Some, like myself, were even in their first year, one living at home and right near the school.

Her mother would have us for dinner, but we only felt lucky, never hovered over. To this day I make one of Dorothy's best dessert recipes, her apple crisp-that's almost 60 years! She and her husband were both bridge players, and there was always bridge if four or more were gathered. We loved to play such a diverse and always challenging game and conversation never ceased except when the actual bidding was going on. I can't remember anyone taking the game or themselves so seriously that they weren't fun to be with. I had the memory of a bridge group my mother had played in for over 50 years-1920s-1960s, roughly. Never did I think that one day that would be us, even surpassing their years!

Edie was a true friend and mentor to those of us that were new. I remember her walking into my classroom one day with a very serious look on her face and saying, "I believe justifiable homicide is in order".

My third-grade students, who were working quietly at the time, wondered why I burst out laughing. She, too, had a roomful of 8 year-olds (over 30 always in those days); what one might call a "charming challenge", but stick to the curriculum WE did, with the result that learn the curriculum THEY did.

Hilda, our principal, was a tough task master, but a real educator. I learned so much from her! I'm sure the others would agree. She was intellect, scientist, musician and administrator all rolled into one. How could the whole school not benefit from her knowledge-based management?

Edie won't be playing bridge this Friday night. She's home with husband, Pete and son, Steve. Guess it will be the single ladies. Jung and I both had roommates and while neither of them cared about or knew bridge, one or the other would always make the foursome complete.

Later, however, Edie was a regular, as son, Steve, was older now and needed less mothering. Edie loved the game and we were such comrades. Edie lost Pete way too early to an untimely death, making her a widow for far too long. Son Steve's marriage came apart as well, taking Edie's only grandchild to another town. Her noble manner in enduring all these losses was a good lesson in strength to all those of us who were younger. She also later had a bout with breast cancer and I was available, when possible, to be with her at Stanford Hospital, a doctor's office or at her home. I found her to be amazingly stoic and always positive!

Our personal, close relationship continued through our daughter, Else. We had asked Edie to be her "Godmother" when she was baptized in 1969 and although we were in Georgia and away from Edie, she was flattered, and agreed to be so and their relationship continued.

Else would come down from San Francisco where she lived about 30 years later, even, to see Edie for very brief visits. I can remember with fondness one such visit when we met up in a shopping center parking lot about 16-18 years ago. Else told Edie that she was in love with her Frenchman. Both of them were joyous, daughter and Godmother! Edie's cancer returned, spread to her bones, and she suffered until the early 2000s when the cancer won. What a loss to all who had known and loved her!

A more quiet, refined and low-key mother, Athena, often joined us within a few years of our start. She had had several teaching jobs early in her marriage and had come to our school a couple of years after I had left to join my husband. That was 1970 and she was teaching sixth grade next to Liza, also a bridge player and sixth-grade teacher. Athena's growing children, Caroline and Roddie were still at home and being a widowed mother made her a full-time teacher/mother. I always admired her "pluck" as I got to know her better and better when I returned. I still hold her in such high esteem.

Athena was descended from early Americans; I think from New Jersey or Pennsylvania and had come west to California with her husband, Paul, who had been accepted to Bolt Law school in Berkeley to follow his chosen career path. Oh yes, it was Paul who was from Pennsylvania and Athena from New Jersey. They had met in college in Pennsylvania, coming to California in 1956. He left Bolt and bolted into other things, even serving in the Air Force and working for a couple of different oil companies. Roddie was born in 1959 and had some developmental problems as he moved through his toddler years.

My understanding is that it was speculated at the time to maybe have been caused by the mother, Athena, after her having taken thalidomide during pregnancy. Daughter Caroline was born in 1964. Their father, Paul, was tragically killed in an auto accident in 1969. This must have required particular strength on Athena's part because Roddie's disabilities needed to be monitored and Caroline was only five years of age! She supported her children in every sense, always keeping them close to extended family.

Athena even entertained us with grace and dignity; part of her heritage I always thought. She was not that "into" bridge and was self-critical in that regard, but really seemed to benefit from the strong camaraderie. Her life when we knew her had come with huge challenges and yet she moved through it with aplomb; even participating in a telephone "hotline" for troubled teens; always giving of herself, even to this day. What an amazing friend and a physical beauty, too.

When she had to sell the family home, she was able to get into a new desirable condominium, so we, of course had some amazing Friday nights there over the years. She still lives there-now with her daughter Caroline, now single and assisting both HER college graduate daughter and her senior mother. Yes, we still played bridge there until recently. Good memories and ALWAYS BRIDGE!

Roddie, Athena's son continued to present challenges, through special schools, a variety of living arrangements and even issues of his wanting to change his gender. I recall Athena gently advising him to dress "normally" when with the family, especially when his sister's young children were present.

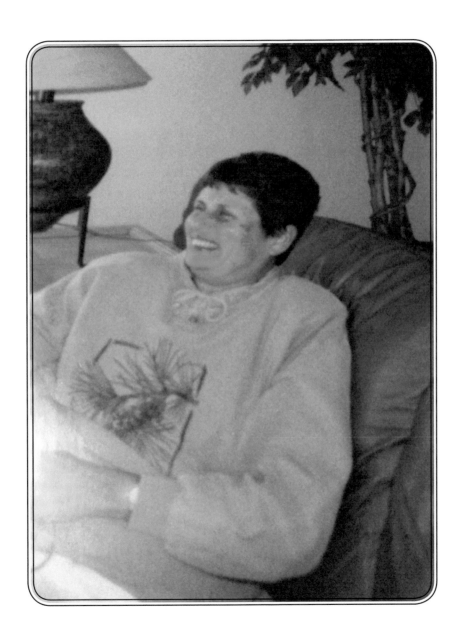

CHAPTER 2

*Y*ung and I both liked to cook and I guess were better at it than most, so we hung out in the kitchen together no matter whose house we were in over the years. In the early days we both visited each other's family homes. Yung was from a small town in Kings County, California, the daughter of immigrants from China and one of 12 children, many of whom (including Yung) had university degrees. I think they had to go to Chinese school on Saturdays to keep up their Cantonese, but spoke perfect English and preferred that. Mr. Lee, Yung's father ran a local grocery store and a couple of her brothers were added in, keeping the store going. I was fascinated by our differences in culture and had so much admiration for what she and her brothers and sisters had accomplished, to say nothing of her parents before them. Think of it. This was almost a century ago! I was so lucky when she took me to her family home to experience not only the different culture, but also such a huge family, many of whom were married and with their own children by then, about 1964, I believe. Yung spoke a Chinese phrase to me when we sat down to the dinner table and told me it meant, "Don't stand on ceremony". She emphasized that I might go without if I didn't help myself to the yummy dishes on the table.

Her mother, truly the matriarch, sat at the head of the table, but spoke no English as I recall and was strongly, but happily still keeping her "children" in line! If I remember correctly, each of the daughters/daughters-in-law had brought a dish for the meal.

I got to do that more than once and then Jung came to Altadena, California to stay with my mom and dad. She brought coveted "bird's nest soup" from her mother to mine and I was a bit afraid that my mom would screw it up, so to speak, when I saw her amazement and heard her ask Yung questions about it. Yung happily filled her in on the sparrow's nest and how they prepare it. I'm sure Mother related to Yung that she had played in the same bridge group for almost 50 years.

Yung was, and is, a huge San Francisco Giants fan and in the early 60's, Bobby Bonds was a player who had enrolled his boys in our elementary school. I got to know both Barry and Bobby Jr., as I returned to the same school after they became students there. Barry was an active and enthusiastic student who played such an amazing four-square game on the playground at recess that he had trouble returning to class on time. During PE, no matter what we played, we could see that he was a gifted athlete.

I indirectly benefitted from Barry because he helped me to keep classroom things organized in the established classroom I came to as a "long-term substitute". I think it was 1971 and then 8 or 9-year old Barry knew exactly where everything was located and how the curriculum was structured. The district was involved in an early experimental curriculum from, I think, Stanford Research Institute. It was called Project Plan. Each student had an individualized lesson plan and it was hard for the arriving teacher to pick it all up and effectively run with it.

Barry was very helpful to me in this regard; all voluntarily! Brother Bobby Jr. ended up being on my son Josh's soccer team in AYSO. Good boys, both the Bonds. and their mother, Pat was always working hard on their behalf when their father, Bobby, was away with the team.

Yung continued to be a faithful Giants fan, but I scolded her soundly when she told me that being a longtime season ticket holder (the longest?) she was asked to be in a publicity shot on the field when the new ballpark opened. Though she was standing right next to Barry, she didn't even mention to him that she had been his second-grade teacher!!!

The blending of our cultures and building of our relationship has never wavered and has continued for almost 60 years, my star student from UC Berkeley, strong teacher, great friend. I truly wish everyone this depth and quality of friendship. I also wish my bridge acumen was as advanced as hers. It's an old wish, but worth striving for. ALWAYS BRIDGE!

CHAPTER 3

In 1966 I married my long time/long distance boyfriend, Gary, with the encouragement of all these colleagues and some not yet referenced. Gary was finishing his college degree and planning to join the Air Force. I had met him when he was a Marine and I was in Hawaii with friends to celebrate our having finished our undergraduate programs at the University of California at Santa Barbara. That's also when I got my teaching certificate and accepted my first teaching assignment. Gary returned home to Oakland when he separated from "The Corps" as he called it, and promptly signed up at Cal Berkeley and then San Francisco State, where he majored in Mandarin Chinese. When I told my parents we'd be heading for Guam when his pilot training was complete, my mother thought sure it meant that Gary was going "to defect". She was actually worried and didn't really know him yet. I was the one who knew that he really just wanted to fly, but Chinese language and an airplane? It was hard for Mother to wrap her head around it. She just knew that her daughter was going to marry this guy and kicked into her "proper" mode. She, by the way, was the earliest "strong woman" in my life: born in 1902 of immigrant parents, each with his own story.

Of course I had to leave my comfy assignment with the third grade and my dear friends, but somehow I always knew I'd be back—back from South Georgia, then Texas, and finally Guam. After all, there was a war going on.

Our daughter, Else was born a southern belle in Georgia and our son, Josh was born on Guam almost two years later, just before we "got out" and headed home for our civilian life. Soon I was back teaching at the same school. Hilda knew I was home and called me about a long-term substitute job she had (yes, even in the same grade) replacing a teacher who was leaving to give birth. There was no such thing as "maternity leave" for teachers in those days. I think it was 1971. That's when Barry Bonds was so helpful to me.

Although I had played bridge with the other officers' wives from time to time, I was glad to get back to the old Friday night group when they included me. When I was away, another amazing bridge player got the group to playing duplicate a la ACBL and I was broken into playing a more serious game with boards. We played a bastardized version I think, but I believe Liza was right. It was more challenging for all. We played at least once a month for sure and took turns hosting the group. ALWAYS BRIDGE!

CHAPTER 4

Early in the game, about 1964, a human dynamo was hired by Hilda to teach fifth grade, and we all so welcomed the infusion of energy when Betsy was on staff and at the bridge table! She's been a joyous personality to us on and off over the years and even came back to us (a figure of speech only, as she was only living at a distance and never really away).

Betsy's intensity at the bridge table implied that most of us just didn't get it. But she was still always willing to be with us, more youthful, but probably appreciative of the solidity of our friendship: maybe even the wisdom and maturity of some members. Her slate was wide open, but not without challenges that had nothing to do with bridge!

Betsy married Doc in 1968; a veterinarian by trade and a very fun professional. My kids enjoyed him as much as I did. I've never forgotten, though, when several of us went to Lake Tahoe for a weekend and stayed in Yung's sister's vacation house. Yes, it was a Friday after a work week for us all. I was so tired (had two young kids at home by now, too, remember) that I didn't even want to join the others in a run to the casinos and opted to stay home. Doc didn't feel up to par (an old term of my mother's) so he stayed back as well. We had some great conversation and then he announced to me that he had diagnosed himself with ALS, Lou Gehrig's Disease, and would be seeing a doctor the following week to have it confirmed. I was in shock, but sworn to secrecy, telling only husband, Gary, when we got home.

Doc had been accurate in his self-diagnosis and he and Betsy began to deal with it. His deterioration seemed quite rapid to me. The last time I saw him, he was in the hospital from which he never left. Son, Art was born to Betsy and Doc in 1977 and Doc passed away in 1978. So hard! Betsy moved with small baby to Pacific Grove and bought a home near to her parents, who helped in many ways to make things better. I always loved when she came back to our area with baby Art to visit.

My children felt joy they had lost with Doc's death by supervising Art in his bouncy chair hanging from the door jam. That little guy was the bounciest ever! My daughter, Else, especially had benefitted from a book titled Hello Sun that helped youngsters put death into a more spiritual place. She read it many times after learning that Doc had died.

In the late 80s or early 90s several of us would be down in Pacific Grove at Betsy's house to visit and play bridge. Before we could do much of either, we had to set up the many duplicate boards for the groups she would be coordinating (as Director?). But, hey, we could still talk, shuffle, deal, stack boards, talk and eat. When we were finished, we played bridge, caught up and had a great time with Miss ACBL! ALWAYS BRIDGE.

CHAPTER 5

Lizzie was a well-respected "Special Ed" teacher in our district. This much-needed aid for children at the K-8 level has had many incarnations and thus, names, but so many fortunate students in our district had benefitted from Lizzie's always reasoned, but gentle but positive understanding of their needs. Lizzie was a single mom who doggedly supported her NOT educationally disadvantaged daughter, Carrie. I, personally, benefitted by having Carrie in my fifth-grade class on a different campus from where her mother taught.

I remember strongly the day, long after our respective daughters had moved on in school, that I met up with Lizzie in the parking lot of the school district offices, where I worked on my district level assignment and "mentor teacher" designation, and she told me she had committed to marriage. What a joy, but I didn't even know she was "seeing someone" (also language from my mother's era). Ralph was in her hiking group, so they had gotten to know each other's stories while "on the trail" of the San Francisco peninsula. Ralph's grown family were living locally, so there was now a larger, blended family. Great for both, but likely, mostly for Carrie and Lizzie. I knew how hard Lizzie worked to have things right for Carrie and was always grateful that Carrie's grandparents were close by until their deaths, for the support that a single mom needed.

The only difficult things now are what all us seniors are experiencing with regards to keeping healthy and viable, with glitches along the way and Lizzie has experienced several physical traumas in recent days! She has bounced back with her usual resilience though. We all are glad that she and Ralph have moved into a more "sensible" home (Doesn't that just sound like a bunch of teachers?) that caters to seniors and is still all they need.

The concern always disappears when we are together for bridge. ALWAYS BRIDGE and/or a special "out for lunch" occasion, as happened very recently. That occasion, by the way, is when all chose their anonymous ID for this story.

CHAPTER 6

In 1965, another strong, gifted teacher was hired to our district-to a K-8 school that was one of (if not THE) original elementary schools in our town. Circe started out teaching the first grade. I remember meeting her early on in her first -grade classroom. I had resigned my position and was waiting for Gary to go through pilot training, officer training and flight school before I joined him. The district superintendent called me in and asked me to take a "long-term sub" job, my first one, and also be teacher support for a couple of newer teachers who, it was determined, needed it. A few years later, Circe was a middle school math teacher and counsellor. As I remember, this change came when our elementary schools were changed to K-5, so our middle schools both became 6-8 to accommodate our student population at that time. Circe's school was 6-8 with a divided campus, the elementary schools, now K-5.

By this time, 'Circe was playing bridge in the Friday night group that I'd be leaving and we were getting closer and closer. She had gone from first-grade to fourth grade teacher and then to counsellor and math mentor at the 6th-8th grade part of the school. She was an excellent teacher and it was felt that she could easily be the one to handle and inaugurate the digital revolution which was about to happen. Circe was married to Harry in 1969. He worked at Fairchild and later at Intel.

In my newer fifth grade job at a different school in the district, I had worked on problem solving with students and was also aware that learning styles would be changing rapidly when computers became routine in our daily lives. Curriculum would now be approached in a completely different manner. Circe and I each found some funding an each bought an original TRS 80 computer from Radio Shack for our respective classrooms. We used bridge night to consult each other about how we were using them. The kids at my level primarily played a game called WORM and I prepared some lessons on the binary system. There were also a couple of more challenging word games, but the idea was to let the children explore usage. I wanted to learn more and remembered that several of us district teachers had a field trip to Stanford Research Institute to learn about these room-sized mother computers. Fortunately our learning curve got to level out because Apple was now charging forward and we would be beneficiaries of its Apples for the Classroom program in which a desktop II E was put in every classroom through THE KIDS CAN'T WAIT-Computers in The Classroom program. A desktop was now placed in every classroom in California, some elsewhere, and before long, each school had a computer lab, where the digital divide was only between older teachers and their students, who were enthusiastically embracing the opportunities the new "machines" provided. "Technology, here I come!" the students seemed to say.

Some of my "gifted" students were getting so proficient on the Apple II E in our classroom that I would find messages for myself on MY files on our classroom computer and felt that I had to talk to them about privacy and hacking.

I have a more personal connection, even. Gary was recruited from his job in US Customs to become Apple's first Corporate Customs Administrator. It was exciting to be at the apex of such an innovative endeavor!

Circe's son, Seth, was born in 1975. He was known to each of us and was a joy. We followed all his school achievements and attended his Bar Mitzva. Though he could have, as an only child, been a spoiled Jewish son, instead he was a smart, well-rounded natural kid. I think I most loved that he chose to play the tuba in the school band! Maybe he used that fact in his accepted application to University of Southern California. We were all proud of him.

His father, Harry was successful in Silicon Valley and occasionally substituted at bridge when we needed him on a Friday night at his house. Sadly, he died a highly unexpected and ignominious death in 2004 in their Tahoe condominium where he had gone for a ski weekend.

Circe carried on nobly, organizing her surprising new lifestyle and helped Seth deal with his father's death and absence.

Seth graduated from USC, met a girl he loved, (all in Southern California) and was married. When Seth's wife became pregnant, Circe hoped they would move to Northern California so that she could help with and be with the expected grandchild. When they were in Northern California, in 2013 I think it was, Seth got a severe headache and the emergency room follow-up detected a cancerous neuroblastoma on his brain. After many months of treatment and a visit to his aging grandmother in Florida who was never to know he was ill, Seth succumbed in 2014. One can't even imagine this second loss for Circe!

She grieved, of course, but also bucked up and now retired, took charge of her life immediately, golfing, tutoring (as she had done for a long time) and played bridge; yes, ALWAYS BRIDGE!

I never saw even a glimpse of her feeling sorry for herself. She's still a model of positivity and a joy to be with, even to the point of using her clever sense of humor regularly or inquiring about what book titles would be appropriate for her long-time tutee. She also added some bridge lessons and a few tournaments. I hope she doesn't get too good for me to play with! ALWAYS BRIDGE!

I just learned that she's gathered enough points to become an ACBL Master. Good job, Circe!

CHAPTER 7

Catherine is the newest member of our bridge group and has not been a lifetime bridge player. She was asked to join us when one of our members passed away and she showed an interest. I had known Catherine for a long time and can't remember how she got started with us, but she dared to show an interest in "our" game; no double entendre intended here.

I team taught with Catherine at one of the smaller schools in our district and we were a good balance for students, as our styles were different, but our focus and dispositions were strong and cheerful. More than one student returned from middle school (most of them could walk home in those days and did so right by the school where their former teachers were working after classes were out for the day). They would reminisce that they had had fun, but learned a lot when under our tutelage. When I queried them about whether or not they had felt prepared, they always responded positively.

A particular interest of students in the fourth and fifth grades is science, natural or otherwise, so we always tried to have hands on, high-interest activities in that area, and of course we had two Apple II E 's in our double classroom!

Another benefit was that this was their year to spend a week at outdoor science camp on the coast. Needless to say, their classroom teachers also attended to supplement and supervise and to deal with any personal issues such as homesickness or hygiene related problems.

We got to know the 'camp with children' routine quite well! I remember at least one year when rather than ride the bus with the children, I took my car, with Catherine, too. I wanted to be able to check-in mid-week with my own children who were home with their father. Once I ended up doing so sooner in the week than I expected because I had to take home a male student who had crossed too many behavior barriers. Some "fun" things were never easy for teachers and other adult supervisors, but then eventually there was Friday night bridge. ALWAYS BRIDGE!

Catherine learned the game quickly and was certainly a pleasant addition to our group! After all, even though a farm girl, basically, from the great Central Valley; yes, another "Valley Girl", she was both Phi Beta Kappa and MENSA. I feel like she always loved our outings to the mountains of Calaveras County where my husband and I have had a vacation home since 1980 and now live permanently in Arnold on the "Highway 4 Corridor" of Calaveras County.

Catherine and her "significant other", Richard are very mobile and often travel to various locales to see and do things of interest. They have toured our county as well as over the Sierra and we have welcomed them here to be with us for interesting conversation.

CHAPTER 8

In 1980-1983 our first vacation home was built for a family vacation cabin by my husband, Gary, who purchased a partially pre-built cabin from Pacific Modern Homes. The pieces and parts arrived on a big truck to our lot and the whole family celebrated. Personal friends came up and helped Gary get started, but by the time the loft was to go up, he was on his own! When I asked how he knew how to complete it, he responded with, "Well, I'm a good reader, aren't I?"

I've always known it takes a lot more than that to complete such a daunting project, but complete it he did and we all four loved our mountain cabin and the retreats that followed.

Even 'the bridge ladies" enjoyed individual visits with us, but eventually we built a more permanent "cabin" where all could come to visit and vacation. That year was 1987. As teens, Josh and Else brought friends and before too many years passed, those folks came less often, but there was ALWAYS BRIDGE! When the bridge ladies came, we usually ate some meals out, some in, took walks, visited sights and YES, kept a running score each time bridge was played. This was always "social bridge" only, so we kept track of the score in order to award a winner and give the lowest score her booby prize; usually the whole dollar she had anted up in the first place

When I finally retired in 1995, Gary, (already newly retired) and I were eager to live full time in the cabin near the Big Trees State Park, so move we did, lock, stock and barrel, to the newest house in the high mountains. The barrel part was significant; not the barrel of a gun, but an old oak barrel that contained a prize rhododendron that my brother-in-law had nurtured and given to me. I felt that it must come, too, so put it and some other plants and items in the back of the U-Haul trailer, hooked up to the car, which followed Gary in the moving van onto Highway #101 to begin our new adventure…35 years after this memoir began.

The aforementioned rhododendron suffered greatly in the open trailer and was almost completely denuded of leaves by the time we arrived "home", yet it thrives today in front of our current home in Arnold, surrounded by others I've added and often is commented upon in the spring by appreciative neighbors out for a walk. Some plant! Maybe it's a metaphor for the strong ladies?

Our new location, plus retirement prompted the Friday night ladies to suggest that my turn for hosting (usually once yearly) could come with a visit from the whole group for a couple of days. Yay! We all wanted to do it, so scheduled it for late that June, 1996, when those who were still teaching would be out for summer break and could come for a couple of weekdays, have some fun, cook and eat and play bridge. ALWAYS BRIDGE!

That year (probably 1996) we had scheduled to go out for lunch and look around a gold rush town in the Mother Lode, but woke, surprisingly to snow, so stayed home and played even more bridge. Was that the same year the toilet overflowed and even ran down the stairs? I was glad we had purchased so many terry bath towels to help with clean-up and had to remind myself to educate the ladies regarding septic tank dos and don'ts!!

The following year, Circe's trunk kept opening and closing, so it seems that for the next 15-18 years we had an event happened to mark our time together. We even began to name some of them to remind ourselves; "the year of the popping trunk", etc.

By our 1998 visit we were in a house we had built on a nice big lot 1000 feet lower in altitude. I had great hopes of a longer season to do some gardening, but realistically we're still in a lovely mixed conifer forest and I try to choose plants that can handle our limited growing season and still look good. The many local deer, rabbits and squirrels really appreciate any gardening I do to supplement their native diet!!!

Early on we drew numbers at the end of each time together in the mountains, not actually numbers, but rather sleeping arrangements and meal responsibilities.

A bunch of teachers can handle organizational things with no problem whatsoever and this worked very well (with a few small exceptions which were respected). I remember that the first or second time in the current house Athena chose to take a sleeping bag onto the back deck and enjoy the mountain air, but came in during the night. She thought it was because of a bear, or possibly mountain lion visit, but I suspect that it was actually a neighbor's dog's curiosity that she was experiencing. We found her on the couch in the morning when we headed for our coffee. She just always hoped later on for one of the single beds or no roommate when she drew. Gary always goes camping for a couple of days so our big bed can accommodate myself and one other. If someone is infirm or has special needs, that bed (and the accompanying Jo supervision) are perfect for that.

One time Betsy was able to join us, as in the old days, because her sister lived in nearby Pinegrove. That way, she could just come over here and play bridge and eat with the old buddies. I don't remember if she stayed the night, too.

An interesting sidelight is that when we cook our meals, we've learned to do things that are less impressive and just as good. I remember the days when several of the ladies brought a cooler or two full of well-planned and prepared goodies to be cooked and/or served, some stopping at the grocery store as they arrived.

We also graduated to two evening meals out and that way, two people could bring bridge table snacks, one, beverages and the rest share cooking breakfasts. With these ladies it's always been a flexible team endeavor, supportive of our own fun and ALWAYS BRIDGE!

A few years ago, Mary, who had slept in the big bed with me so no one would be bothered by the noise of her C-Pap breathing assistance, came into the kitchen in the morning and sat on a stool at the counter where the designated breakfast people were working on our coming delicacies. Within minutes, she swooned and fell to the floor. Three of us kicked into gear, checked her vitals and called 911. We had moved her to a chair close by, but then wanted her to be lying on the floor for the EMT'S. Catherine showed me how they had once learned to move her elderly mother and that is what we did. Three highly competent EMT'S worked with Mary and asked us a lot of questions. We had already scrounged her handbag and medications from the master bedroom and then they told us they would put her in the ambulance as soon as she was stable.

Meanwhile, one young EMT asked how she was moved to the floor on the carpet in the living room. Obviously, he had glanced around the room at the bathrobe-clad old ladies and he said he was amazed, asking "Who got her to here? I merely told him we were long-retired teachers who knew how to do "stuff".

Mary stayed the night at a local rural hospital and her daughter came the next day to pick her up. Even though Mary was the eldest, we all had come to realize that we were somewhat tempting fate with our annual mountain event for bridge. More recently a smaller number has made the trek and last year, sadly, we did not convene.

CHAPTER 9

When we came full time to our mountain abode, I did three things to benefit myself. I signed on to volunteer as a classroom helper at the local elementary school, joined a book group and played in a social bridge group who played two tables twice a month, alternating hostesses as I was accustomed to doing before. Those were all good choices and fed me well.

The mother of a young man who built our second house and would also build our third, was an avid duplicate bridge player and asked me to sub in a group she played in. She later asked me to replace, permanently (whatever that means at our age) in that group, a player who was leaving.

Their members were aging, too, and occasionally someone had to relocate for medical reasons. I now play four times a month, regularly, with some substituting in other groups when needed. ALWAYS BRIDGE and a big selection of women who fit the general theme of this memoir.

Two of those women stand out in particular-woman strength being what built them. The first of those two, Diane, is a quiet, controlled person of few words. In other words, she does not do the "blathering" that some of us do, both at the table and away. No wonder I respect her so! Not just for that quality but that she is also a wonderfully caring personal companion, sensitive in conversation, particularly one-on-one. She is an excellent bridge player as well.

Diane and her husband, Don, relocated to mountain country from the all too hectic Bay Area in 2001, after having raised their family and working there. They were married in Carson City, Nevada in 1951. Ann was born in 1952 and Dave, in 1963.

Now, in 2001, Diane and Don looked forward to having downsized to a small local condominium so that they could enjoy skiing and other seasonal highlights of our area and also be unencumbered for travel, sometimes of the international type.

Don was retired and Diane worked in a marketing/editing job. Both their son and daughter, as well as grand-children (one of whom they had championed all his life and been very close to) live out of the area.

They had the good life; reading, keeping up with politics, traveling and enjoying friends and family until both of them had physical issues. By the time I met Diane over the bridge table, I learned of Don's back (or was it neck?) problems. He had had spinal issues starting in 2007. They persisted and he had to take strong pain medications to which he did not react well, as I understand it. Diane had her physical issues, too, and both of them had surgeries. Diane had kidney surgery and was unable to care for Don at home when he needed his surgery, so he was in Colorado for his surgery!

In 2015 Don, not recovering that well, was placed in a long-term care facility in a rural town roughly 30 miles from here. Diane made the drive several times a week to be with him, then, once a week and while he was not improving, she, too was getting less strong physically.

Don passed away in 2017 and while Diane was dealing with that loss and staying at her sister's out of the area, she had a fall. She sustained several broken bones and was not recovering as well as expected. Diane went to Stanford University Hospital to have more intensive evaluation and was found to have Parkinson's Disease! What a blow!

I'm sure there was lots of discussion with family as to the next step, but my strong friend, Diane, determined that she should stay where she was, in our small, but peaceful area and close to many bridge-playing friends. She would need to have her condo modified as she grew less able stand or walk.

Her talented brother did an amazing job of lowering counters, installing "grab" poles, removing the master bathroom door for access from the bedroom, closing off the upstairs which wouldn't be used anyway and could keep heat in the area in which she would function.

Now that Diane is pretty much confined to a wheelchair, one can see how far-sighted this plan was. The most amazing adjustment to me, is the lift he installed that allows Diane to get to ground level without any stairs to worry about. We use it when we transport her to get groceries or whatever. She moves about in her own kitchen while seated and still prepares good stuff to eat. If we are to play bridge at a place that's difficult for her to get in or out of, we go to her house instead. Her level of independence is admirable! She asks for help getting to market or even the airport, only when necessary. Several of us enjoy picking her up, tossing her wheelchair in the back and wheeling in to "wherever" to play bridge. ALWAYS BRIDGE!

CHAPTER 10

The other "mountain woman" I referred to earlier is Shirley. She and Foster first came to our area on "The Highway 4 Corridor" in 1979. For Shirley it was weekends while she was still teaching in the Bay Area. For Foster it was leaving his job with which he was disenchanted and resettling in the mountains where he began to buy up properties and design houses, including the attractive one in which they are both retired for the past almost 20 years.

Shirley was born in Oakland, California, the third child to her parents who were tragically killed in the crash of a private plane while on their way to a wedding in Reno, Nevada. Shirley was only 13. I don't know how old her brother and sister were!

Her aunt and uncle convinced the recently widowed grandmother to come to the house and raise the three children of this tragedy until they were adults.

This was particularly helpful to the children because their parents had been on the go a lot and weren't such effective disciplinarians as she. Do I detect another strong woman here?

Shirley was graduated from UC Berkeley (as was her brother) and began her teaching career in 1955 on the San Francisco Peninsula before her marriage to Foster. Upon the birth of her first son (they had three sons), she stayed home (as was more typical at that time), re-entering her profession to become a very valuable educator in her school district, now on the east side of the bay. I would comfortably call her a gifted teacher, with special certification as a reading specialist and leader in many areas. She was also a mentor teacher for 10 years, allowing many teachers (and thus, students) to benefit from her skills; 36 years, all told, to California youngsters and I'm sure it was always with her very positive disposition. Yes, a woman of great strength!

Shirley retired to her mountain abode and was available to play bridge in various existing groups and also Then to help those in the learning stages, even coordinated a group learning to trade party bridge for the more structured duplicate bridge of ACBL. I always feel fortunate to have her cheerful disposition at a table at which I play. ALWAYS BRIDGE!

Shirley's Foster, now 92 years old, deals with macular degeneration, making any day a challenge for him, and even more so for Shirley, who takes over whenever Foster can't see something and, of course, she has to do the driving for shopping, medical appointments, etc.

I don't think any of us hears her complain or whine. She's so stoic! I, personally have no idea how she stoically handled the shocking news of the death of one of her three adult sons. He lost his life in a diving accident in Monterey Bay only 8 or 9 years ago. I imagine a mode of "always bridge" plans and play serve her well as distraction. Her strength prevails.

CHAPTER 11

While missing my "original" group plus replacements, I was still going to the San Francisco Bay Area once a month with one of them as hostess. I stayed all night after bridge, usually with Circe or Yung and Doug, where sometimes we would watch part of a ball game while preparing food, most often staying in their comfortable kitchen/family room. Yung and Doug are still in their lovely home on the coast south of San Francisco. The last few years have Yung staying close to home to be sure that Doug, several years her junior, even, and also with Parkinson's Disease, is well cared for and, I'm very sure, well fed!

Sometimes I stay at our daughter's house in San Francisco. These trips were invaluable for me to keep those original connections with the same strong old broads as we all age. Unfortunately, one time recently, on one of those overnight outings…one where some of us even attended a San Francisco Giants game, my car lost its transmission on the highway on the way home! It was a pretty traumatic experience and I feel lucky to have escaped death even, so am now reluctant to drive alone that same route and distance for one of these rendezvous. I'll try to coordinate a couple of visits with any trips Gary and I take to San Francisco to be with our daughter, son-in-law and two amazing grandsons.

I've often mentioned to my daughter, Else, to be sure to have a cadre of special gals she's close to so she will always feel affirmed and supported by these types of women whose company she so enjoys. Being a strong woman herself, she is well aware of this paradigm. I try to refrain from too much philosophical analysis, but will let the reader do this.

Meanwhile, along with the two previously mentioned friends, Shirley and Diane, we good old broads press on and there's ALWAYS BRIDGE!

AFTERWORD

In telling these stories, it's been my intention to honor and memorialize these women, my friends, getting the facts as accurate as possible. I couldn't be more lucky or proud, but would also hope that the readers reflect on these stories and identify the women in their lives with a similar appreciation. They may not play bridge, but they're there!

Each character chose her own anonymous ID and that of family, where appropriate. Only the deceased were not able to do that and are referred to here mostly with their given names.

2019

AUTHOR BIOGRAPHY

Linda J. Palmer was a longtime educator in a K–8, small
school district on the San Francisco Peninsula.

Printed in the United States
By Bookmasters